The Scandinavian Cookbook

by
Dr. Duane R. Lund

Featuring
Traditional and Modern Recipes
From
NORWAY   SWEDEN
DENMARK   FINLAND

Distributed by
Adventure Publications
P. O. Box 269
Cambridge, Minnesota 55008

First Printing, 1992
Second Printing, 1992
Third Printing, 1994
Fourth Printing, 1997
Fifth Printing, 2000
Sixth Printing, 2003
Seventh Printing, 2005

Printed in the United States of America
by
Lund S&R Publications
Staples, Minnesota 56479

ISBN-10: 0-934860-88-2
ISBN-13: 978-0-934860-88-8

DEDICATION
To my four Scandinavian-born grandparents:
Ellen Lund
John Lund
Louise Anderson
Andrew Anderson
They gave me an appreciation for all things Scandinavian —
especially Scandinavian foods!

TABLE OF CONTENTS

CHAPTER II
BREADS, ROLLS, PASTRIES AND PANCAKES

CHAPTER III
SOUPS AND BROTHS

CHAPTER IV
STEWS

CHAPTER V
FISH

CHAPTER VI
MEATS

CHAPTER VII
VEGETABLES, CASSEROLES AND SIDE DISHES

CHAPTER VIII
DESSERTS

INTRODUCTION

The Scandinavian Cookbook features both traditional and modern day recipes from Norway, Sweden, Denmark and Finland. Approximately 90% of the recipes were collected by the author during his visits to the Scandinavian countries over more than twenty years.

Some of the recipes are identified with a particular country but the vast majority can be found in similar form in several or all of the countries.

Every effort has been made to state the recipes as simply and as clearly as possible. It should be possible for non-Scandinavians or amateur cooks to produce gourmet quality dishes.

ENJOY!

FOR DIET-CONSCIOUS COOKING

- Margarine may be substituted for butter. Although the taste may not be exactly the same, the food will still be delicious.
- Replace cooking oil and fat with non-stick cooking spray.
- Remove the skin from poultry and trim away all fat from poultry and other meats before cooking. Choose leaner cuts.
- Skim fat from soups, gravies and stews.
- Use lower calorie dairy products.

CHAPTER I

THE SMÖRGASBORD

The name "Smörgasbord" is used world-wide and applies to most any buffet featuring a variety of dishes. The original Swedish smörgasbord was more like an elaborate display of hors d'oeuvres, featuring among other things a variety of open-faced sandwiches, usually cut relatively small and in a variety of shapes. When eaten as a meal, it was customary to visit the table several times, choosing a few things each visit, perhaps beginning with herring, then moving to salads, smoked fish, sandwiches, cheeses, pickles, meatballs, sausages, and eggs.

The recipes which follow are true to the original Swedish concept and most any of them, even by themselves, will serve as tasty hors d'oeuvres.

SANDWICH OPTIONS

Use a variety of breads cut into different shapes and sizes. Leave them open-faced (no bread on top). Trim away the crust. Crisp breads and wafers are also appropriate.

Smoked Meat

Use thin slices of dried beef (Scandinavians often use smoked reindeer). Butter the bread. Add a layer of mayonnaise mixed with finely chopped hard-boiled* eggs. Top with the meat. Garnish with a little circle or dab of the mayonnaise-egg mixture on the meat.

---

*Bring to a boil, turn off the heat and let sit for 20-minutes or so for hard-cooked.

Shrimp

Use tiny, fresh-cooked shrimps. Stir together the shrimps and either red or white tartar sauce until the shrimps are well coated. Spoon a generous layer on the bread and top with two or three uncoated shrimps and perhaps a sprig of parsley.

Smoked Fish and Cream Cheese

(Smoked eel is a traditional favorite.)

Chop the smoked fish into tiny flakes. Stir together 3 parts cream cheese and one part mayonnaise. Thoroughly blend equal portions of the fish and cheese-mayonnaise, forming a spread. Garnish with a sprig of dill.

Herring and Potatoes

Use pickled herring and small boiled potatoes. Chop the herring quite fine. Slice the potatoes. Butter the bread. Add a leaf of lettuce and/or a little mayonnaise. Cover with sliced potatoes. Top with the herring.

Caviar

Most any variety of caviar (sturgeon, salmon, whitefish or cod) is appropriate. Use very small pieces of bread or use crackers. The caviar may be used by itself or with finely chopped hard-boiled eggs or cold scrambled eggs. Butter the bread first.

Ham

Ham, of course, is good by itself, especially on dark breads; but for a different taste treat, add sliced prunes or raisins. A very thin spread of a gourmet mustard or mayonnaise may be used instead of (or with) butter.

Cheeses

Traditional smorgasbords feature a variety of cheeses by themselves, usually of the stronger varieties. Of course, cheese also makes a tasty sandwich. Milder cheeses (such as Swiss or cheddar) are better with bread. Butter the bread and then add a little mayonnaise and/or a piece of lettuce. Top with the cheese. Thinly sliced cucumbers and/or sliced radishes also go well with cheese sandwiches, also sliced green or ripe olives.

Salted* Herring

Flavor 1 cup of sour cream with 1 T dill seed (or 2 T chopped fresh dill) and 1 T minced onion. Cut the herring in pieces to fit the pieces of bread. Spread the sour cream mixture over the herring. Garnish with dill sprig.

Full Loaf Sandwich

This will make a spectacular centerpiece for your smörgasbord display. Use a whole loaf of unsliced bread. Place the loaf on end and make three or four cuts the full length of the loaf, thus making 4 or 5 slices of bread the length of the loaf. If you can slice the bread thinner without breaking the slices, you may try for even more slices! Now reconstruct the loaf but with a *different* filling on each slice. Any of the above may be used. When the loaf has been reconstructed, cover it completely (top and all 4 sides) with cream cheese, applied like icing on a cake. Garnish the loaf creatively. One possibility would be sliced green or ripe olives or sliced radishes.

To serve the gigantic sandwich, simply slice as you would a loaf of bread, being careful to hold it together (perhaps with a spatula) while transferring the slices to your guests' plates.

Pickled Herring

1½ pounds salted** herring fillets
¾ cup sugar
½ cup vinegar
2 medium onions, sliced
1 bay leaf
10 allspice (whole)
1 cup water

Soak the herring in cold water overnight. Cut into serving-size chunks.

Combine all other ingredients. Place the herring chunks in a glass container and cover with the mixture. Refrigerate at least 24 hours before serving.

*Pickled herring may also be used.
**Fresh herring may be used, in which case soaking will not be necessary.

Other Variations of Pickled Herring

Use the same basic recipe and procedure as previous page but try some of these substitutions:

wine for water
sour cream for water
white and/or black peppercorns for the allspice

Or these additions:

a sprig of dill or 1 T dill seed, or
¼ cup catsup or chili sauce

Pickled Pike

Fillet the fish as you would a walleye — don't worry about the bones. Cut fish into small (herring-size) pieces. Wash.

Prepare a brine solution by adding one cup of salt (preferably pickling salt) to four cups of water.

Step #1: cover the fish pieces with the brine solution and let stand overnight.

Step #2: wash off the pieces of fish and soak in white vinegar three to four days.

Step #3: drain, rinse and place in jars (pint size is most convenient).

Prepare a pickling solution as follows:

To two cups of vinegar (if you like to use wine in cooking, use one cup of wine and one cup of vinegar) add:

one chopped onion (not fine)
one sliced lemon
2 T mustard seed (level)
1¾ cup sugar
4 bay leaves
5 whole cloves
1 T peppercorns (level)
5 or 6 small red peppers
1 T whole allspice

Bring the solution to a boil, then cool and pour over the fish.

Step #4: pour the pickling solution over the fish pieces you have already packed in the jars (fairly tightly). Cover and refrigerate at least three to four days before serving.

Five to six pounds of cleaned and cut-up northerns will yield approximately one gallon of pickled fish.

Pickled Freshwater Fish #2

Cut 5 pounds of fish into "herring size" chunks. Cover with cold water. Stir in 1 cup of pickling salt and refrigerate for 2 days.

After 24 hours, wash the fish pieces thoroughly and drain on paper towel.

In a stone crock or large jar, place the fish, 1½ cups sugar, the thin slices of three large onions, 4 tablespoons pickling spices and 2 bay leaves.

Cover with white vinegar and gently stir the ingredients together.

Refrigerate for another 2 days.

Fish is now ready to eat and may be divided into smaller jars, but try to give each jar a fair share of onions and spices and be sure the fish are covered with white vinegar.

SALADS

No smörgasbord is complete without at least two or three salads.

Herring Salad (sillsallad)

1 large salt herring
1 cup cooked or pickled beets, diced
1¼ cup cooked potatoes, diced
1 cup diced roast beef (or ham)
1 pickle, finely chopped (medium-sweet)
1 apple, medium, peeled and diced
2 T vinegar
1 t vinegar
1/8 t white pepper
1 hard-boiled egg; cut white into strips, mash yolk
¼ cup whipping cream (whip) or ½ cup sour cream

Soak the herring in water overnight. Rinse, remove skin and bones. Chop fairly fine.

Mix herring, diced beets, diced potatoes, diced meat, diced apple, chopped pickle and add vinegar, sugar and pepper.

Turn out on a platter and garnish with mashed egg yolk in center with egg white strips arranged in a spiral around the yolk. You may also add parsley and small, cooked beets for decoration.

Serve with either whipped or sour cream. Some prefer to stir the cream into the salad before it is placed on the platter.

Beet Salad

      3 medium pickled beets, chopped
      1 apple, peeled, cored and diced
      2 potatoes, boiled, cooled and chopped
      1 T chopped onion
      1 cup sour cream
      1 T mustard (prepared)

Combine all ingredients and chill.

Cabbage Salad (white or red)

      2 cups shredded cabbage
      2 T shredded horseradish
      1 cup apple sauce
      2 T onion, minced

Cabbage with Jellies

      2 cups cabbage, shredded
      1 cup preserves (usually lingonberry in Scandinavia)
      Mix thoroughly and chill.

MISCELLANEOUS SMÖRGASBORD DISHES

Whitefish Roe

      2 cups fresh roe
      ½ cup onion, finely chopped
      salt and pepper to taste

Gently mix together all ingredients. Let stand 24 hours refrigerated before serving. Perhaps better on crackers than bread.

Anchovy Eye

      10 anchovy fillets, chopped fine
      4 egg yolks
      3 T onion, minced
      3 T pickled beets, chopped
      2 T finely chopped boiled potato
      3 T capers

Combine all ingredients into small, hamburger-like patties. Sauté (on both sides) in butter.

Miniature Meatballs

½ pound ground beef
½ pound ground pork
1 egg, beaten
½ cup bread crumbs
3 T onion, minced
1 cup light cream (half and half)
1 T salt
½ t powdered allspice
¼ pound butter

Combine all ingredients. Form in small balls (1") and fry in butter. Serve alone or with cocktail sauce.

Mushroom Balls

1 pound fresh mushrooms of your choice, chopped
1 onion, minced
½ cup bread crumbs
2 eggs
3 T flour
½ t salt
½ t pepper
3 T butter

Sauté the mushroom pieces and chopped onion in the butter. Stir in all other ingredients. Mold into 1 inch balls and heat thoroughly (brown) in the butter remaining in the pan (add more butter if necessary).

Liver Paste (paté)

½ pound liver (pork, beef or poultry)
½ pound pork fat
4 anchovy fillets
1 T onion, minced
2 T flour
¼ t salt
¼ t pepper
2 eggs
1 cup cream
3 T butter

Grind and mix together the liver, fat and anchovies. Sauté the onion in the butter. Mix together all ingredients. Place into a well-greased mold or pan. Since this will be baked while floating in a larger pan of water, put no more into the mold than will float! Bake in a pre-heated medium oven — floating the mold or pan in a larger pan of water. After one hour, remove and let cool. Remove from mold and serve. Keep refrigerated.

CHAPTER II

BREADS, ROLLS, PASTRIES AND PANCAKES

Breads and pastries have long been an important part of Scandinavian food tradition. Surely a Swedish smörgasbord is not a "smörgasbord" without bread. And when it comes to pastries, one can order a sweet roll almost anywhere in the world simply by requesting a "Danish".

Traditionally, most Scandinavian breads were dark and made with rye flour. Today in these four countries, white breads and rolls are at least as common as the darker varieties.

Another time-honored tradition is to dip pieces of bread or rolls into gravies or broths served with the meal.

Swedish Rye Bread (limpa) - My Mother's Recipe

        1 stick (½ cup) margarine
        1 cup brown sugar
        ½ cup molasses
        2¾ cups boiling water
        1 t salt
        2 pkg dry yeast
        ½ t sugar
        ¼ cup warm (110⁰F) water
        1 T anise seed
        3 cups rye flour
        3-4 cups white flour

Place margarine, brown sugar and molasses in bowl. Pour boiling water over this mixture. Stir in salt.

Proof yeast with sugar and water until foamy.

Stir above mixtures together. Add anise seed. Mix in flours. Dough will be sticky until it is completely kneaded. Knead until smooth and elastic, 15-20 minutes. Allow to rise in greased, covered bowl until double in bulk. Punch down and separate dough for loaves. Pat into greased pans; cover and allow to rise until nearly double in bulk. Will be soft to the touch; finger will leave impression. Bake at 350°F 45 minutes. Brush with brown sugar syrup.

Cardamom Bread

> 4 cups flour
> ¼ pound butter
> 1½ cups milk
> ½ t salt
> 1 T ground cardamom or 2 T seeds
> ½ cup sugar
> 1 pkg yeast (2 oz)

Melt the butter. Combine milk and melted butter. Place yeast in mixing bowl and add milk-butter mixture. Add salt, cardamom and sugar. Add flour until a workable dough is formed. Work dough until smooth; let rise 10 minutes (in the bowl). Place dough on a flour-dusted table or board. Shape and cut into loaves or buns. Let rise until dough about doubles in volume.

Brush with a beaten egg.

Bake in a hot oven. Loaves will take 15 to 20 minutes; rolls about half that time.

Saffron Bread

Use the same basic recipe as above (for cardamom breads) but eliminate the cardamom. Use a little more butter and before working in the flour add 1 t ground saffron. Saffron is a potent seasoning; be sure it is mixed in evenly and thoroughly. Experience will teach you how much you would like to use. Make into either loaves or buns.

For variety, add raisins (about ¾ cup for the above recipe).

Danish Pastries

Basic recipe for pastry dough:

3 cups flour

1¼ cups milk

1 pkg yeast (1½ oz)

3 T sugar

¼ t salt

1 egg

½ pound butter

Place yeast in mixing bowl. Beat the egg into the milk; add to the bowl along with salt and sugar. Stir in the flour until the dough becomes workable. Place dough on lightly floured board and knead thoroughly. Roll out the dough to about 1/3 inch thickness. Cut the butter into pats and place on half of the area of the sheet of dough. Fold the unbuttered half over the half with butter. Fold once more and then roll to original thickness. Fold again, twice, and roll again. If dough is too sticky or unworkable, refrigerate 15 minutes, then roll again. The dough should now be ready for making pastries of your design.

Fillings:

Nut filling: Chop or roll nuts of your choice until fine. To one-half cup of chopped nuts, add 3 T softened butter and 1/3 cup sugar. Blend thoroughly.

Vanilla filling:

1 cup milk

1 egg yolk

2 T flour

1 T sugar

2 T vanilla sugar

Mix together all ingredients except the vanilla sugar. Simmer about 5 minutes in a sauce pan, stirring continuously. Let cool. Add vanilla sugar (stir in).

Preserves: Use your favorite jams or jellies.

Potato Lefse *

Peel and boil as many potatoes as you need (figuring 1 medium potato for each lefse you plan to make). When potatoes are done, drain, and add a little milk and ¼ pound butter and mash well. For 8 to 10 - 14 inch lefsas:

> 3 cups mashed potatoes
>
> 1 cup flour
>
> ¼ cup heavy cream
>
> 1 T sugar

Mix together all ingredients (like pie crust). Form into 8 to 10 parts and roll thin. Bake on lefse grill until brown; turn and bake the other side.

*Courtesy Avis Sandland, Clearbrook, MN

Swedish Pancakes

> 1 cup flour
>
> 3 cups milk
>
> 4 eggs
>
> 2 T sugar
>
> pinch of salt

Thoroughly blend all ingredients in a mixing bowl. The batter should be quite thin. Spoon batter onto a hot griddle. Turn only once (to prevent toughness).

Variations

1) Pancakes are sometimes served with confectioners sugar on top and/or a great variety of syrups and berries.

2) Another variation is to make large, but thin, cakes and stack them 8 or 10 high with preserves between them. Cut and serve like a torte.

3) Bits of bacon or salt pork may be pre-fried and added to the batter.

Potato Pancakes (4 servings)

> 4 cups grated potatoes
>
> 4 eggs
>
> 3 T flour
>
> 1 t salt

Combine all ingredients thoroughly. Fry in oil or, preferably, bacon grease.

Potato and Carrot Pancakes

> 2 cups potatoes, ground or minced fine
> 2 cups carrots, ground or minced fine
> 2 egg yolks
> 3 T butter
> salt and pepper

Stir the eggs, potatoes and carrots together. Form into balls and then flatten with a spatula. Fry in the butter, browning both sides. Season to taste.

Potato Dumplings

> 8 medium potatoes, peeled and boiled in salted water
> 1 cup flour
> 2 egg yolks
> ½ pound salt pork, chopped
> 1 T allspice
> 1 onion, chopped fine
> 2 T butter
> salt

Rice the boiled potatoes and stir in the egg yolks. After cooling, mix in the flour evenly, forming a dough. Meanwhile, sauté the chopped pork and onion. Make 2-inch dough balls. Push a hole part way through each ball. Fill hole with about 1 T pork-onion mixture. Pull dough over filling. Cover dumplings with water; bring to a boil, then reduce heat and let simmer. Continue cooking 5 minutes after dumplings float to the surface. Dumplings may be served as is or browned in butter.

Rhubarb Dumplings

Make a dough of:

> ½ pound butter (softened)
> 3 T sugar
> 1½ cups flour

Leave in a cool place for 20 minutes. Roll thin.
Make a filling of:

> 2 cups rhubarb, chopped
> 3 T sugar

Cut dough into a half-dozen squares. Place rhubarb in center of each and sprinkle with sugar. Fold the edges over the filling and press together. Bake in a hot oven. Serve topped with whipped cream.

CHAPTER III

SOUPS AND BROTHS

Not only have soups and broths been served traditionally in Scandinavia with the main meal of the day, but soups have been, and remain, a frequent "main course". Because of the importance of soups and broths, many of the recipes are fairly complicated and take a good deal of time to prepare — but they are well worth the effort!

Cabbage Soup (about 8 servings)
> 2 pounds cabbage, cut into bite-size chunks
> ½ pound potatoes, cubed (¼" - ½")
> 3 large carrots, ½ inch sections
> 8 cups of water or pork broth
> ¾ pound pork (roast, salt pork, or ½ pound of bacon)
> 4 T parsley, chopped coarse
> 12 allspice (whole)
> 10 peppercorns
> salt to taste

Place all ingredients except the parsley in boiling water. Let simmer until meat is tender (low heat). If roast pork is used, cut into bite-size chunks. If salt pork is used, cut into ½ inch strips. Pork broth was frequently used in original recipes rather than water. Consommé soup is a modern touch that works well. Replace one of the cups of water with one small can of the soup. If consommé soup is used, be careful about adding too much salt. Sprinkle parsley on each serving.

Fish Soup (5 - 6 servings)

This recipe works well with almost any variety of white-meated fish, including pike.

2 pounds fish, scaled and cleaned

½ pound potatoes, cut into bite-sized chunks

2 medium carrots, sliced

5 tomatoes, blanched and peeled, quartered

1 large onion, sliced

2 T lemon juice

8 peppercorns

2 quarts of water

salt to taste

Cut the cleaned and scaled fish into 2 to 3 inch chunks (original recipes used the heads — there is a lot of good meat in the cheeks). Place all ingredients except the fish in a kettle of cold water. Bring to a gentle boil and cook for about 10 minutes. Add the fish and continue cooking until the fish flakes easily and the vegetables are done. Skim off anything that comes to the surface.

Smoked Fish Soup (6 servings)

Use either saltwater or freshwater fish. Smoked eel was commonly used in original recipes and remains a favorite to this day in all Scandinavian countries.

2 pounds smoked fish

¾ pound potatoes, cut into bite-size chunks

2 medium onions, chopped

salt to taste (other seasonings may be added, such as white pepper, thyme, dill or your favorite)

2 T parsley, chopped

4 T butter

3 cups cream

Boil the potato chunks until done. Meanwhile, sauté the onion in the butter. Using the pan in which you sautéed the onion, add the potatoes, cream and seasonings. Simmer until all ingredients are hot. Serve in shallow bowls over pieces of smoked fish and garnish with the chopped parsley. More modern variations of this recipe call for about 3 T soy sauce.

Nettle Soup (6 servings)

Times were sometimes tough "in the old days" and people often had to "make do" with what nature provided. This soup is quite tasty, however, and is served to this day, particularly in rural homes where nettles are more readily available.

> 6 cups of nettles (young and tender),
>
> 6 cups of water (a more modern touch includes a cube or two of beef bouillon)
>
> 2 T butter
>
> 3 T chives, chopped
>
> 2 T flour
>
> salt and pepper to taste

Cook the nettles in the water or bouillon until tender. Strain out the nettles and chop fine. Return the nettles to the liquid. Bring to a boil, meanwhile stirring the butter and flour together. Add butter-flour to the soup and continue to cook for a few minutes. Season to taste and sprinkle the chives onto each bowl as you serve the soup.

Sometimes served with eggs, usually hard-boiled, sliced.

Pea Soup (6 servings)

Pea soup has long been a favorite throughout Scandinavia. Before the days of freezing and canning, dried peas could be kept almost indefinitely thus making pea soup a frequent dish.

> 2 cups yellow (dried) peas
>
> 7 cups water
>
> ¾ pound salt pork (small chunks or ½ inch strips)
>
> 1 t thyme
>
> 1 T salt

Add one T of salt to the cold water and then add the peas; let them soak overnight (or for about 10 hours). Drain the water, and add new water and another T of salt. Bring to a boil (covered) for a few minutes. Remove from heat and skim off any shells on the surface. Return to heat and let simmer (slow boil) for about a half-hour. Add the salt pork and let simmer until peas are tender (30 -45 minutes). Season to taste with thyme and possibly more salt.

Crayfish Soup (6 servings)

> 2 dozen freshwater crayfish (live)
> 6 cups water (modern recipes call for beef bouillon)
> ½ pound potatoes, quartered
> 2 large onions, chopped
> 3 medium carrots, sliced
> 2 cups white wine
> 1 bay leaf
> 1 cup cream
> 8 peppercorns (white, if available)
> 1 t marjoram
> 3 T butter
> 3 T flour

Sauté the onion in the butter. To 6 cups of water or bouillon, add the spices and the vegetables. Bring to a boil and add the crayfish. Boil for 15 minutes. While the soup cooks for another ten minutes, remove and shell the crayfish tails. Cut tails into two or three pieces. Skim the soup, add the cream and the crayfish tails. Add the flour to the butter you used to sauté the onion. Stir into the soup.

Check for flavor and add seasonings if necessary. Serve hot.

Blood Soups

Blood is not an unusual ingredient in traditional Scandinavian cooking. It is used in sausage, soups and stews. The following recipe is one variation. The vegetables and meat ingredients can be varied.

First, make a stock, using ingredients such as:

> bones from poultry, beef or veal
> > (broken or crushed)
> 2 onions, sliced
> 3 large carrots, chunked
> 2 large potatoes, chunked
> ½ cup celery, chopped small
> 2 cups apples (chunked or just the peelings)
> 6 quarts water
> 2 cups poultry giblets (or other meat)
> some or all of the following seasonings:

2 T salt
2 sticks cinnamon
10 peppercorns
10 allspice (whole)
1 t thyme
1 t marjoram
1 bay (or laurel) leaf
3 T parsley
2 T cloves, whole

Cook all ingredients over low heat for 6 hours. Skim occasionally. Next, prepare the soup (really a broth), thus:

1 quart blood (hog or poultry or mixed)
1 cup flour
2 cups red wine
3 T sugar

During the last hour of simmering the stock, mix the flour into the blood. Let set for the hour. Skim the stock if needed. Bring to a boil. Stir in the flour-blood mixture. When the stock again begins to boil, remove from the heat and stir in the wine and sugar. Strain and serve the broth.

Other ingredients sometimes added include apple juice, prune juice, brandy, syrup and molasses.

Gamebird Broth (6 servings)

2 uncooked carcasses from which the meat has been used for other dishes
2 carrots, chopped fairly fine
2 onions, chopped
1 stalk celery, chopped
1 bay leaf
8 peppercorns
1 t salt
1 quart water (or bouillon)
1 cup sherry (optional)
1 cup cream

Cut the carcasses into several pieces. Place all ingredients in a kettle except the sherry and cream. Bring to a boil and then reduce heat and let simmer for 2 hours. Skim regularly. Strain and add sherry and cream to the liquid; discard solids. Return to heat and remove as it starts to boil. For a brown appearance and spicier flavor, add soy sauce or Kitchen Bouquet.

CHAPTER IV

STEWS

Scandinavians take pride in their excellent stews. As with soups and broths, the recipes are often quite lengthy and take considerable time to produce. Traditional stews often feature fish or wild game. Because Scandinavian countries have been and remain blessed with wild game and an abundance of fresh and saltwater fish, this is only natural.

Veal Stew (4 servings)

> 2 pounds veal roast (may use cheaper cuts, such as neck or brisket)
> 4 potatoes, medium, cubed
> 3 carrots, medium, thick slices
> 1 large onion, sliced
> ½ cup celery, chopped
> 6 peppercorns
> 2 stalks dill, or 2 T dill seed
> salt (1 T for parboiling and 1 t while making stew)

Cut the veal into bite-size chunks (about 1 inch cubes). Cover with water, add a little salt (1 T) and boil for about 20 minutes. Pour off water and rinse meat. Return meat to kettle and add all vegetables and seasonings except the potatoes. Cover with water. When the meat chunks are quite tender, add the cubed potatoes. If at any point the stew seems too thick, add water.

Beef Stew (4 servings)

This recipe works well with venison. Scandinavians also used reindeer and moose.

> 2 pounds beef roast (may use cheaper cuts)
> 4 tomatoes, blanched and peeled
> 4 potatoes, cubed
> 3 carrots, thick sliced
> 1 stalk celery, chopped
> 2 onions, sliced
> 2 T flour
> 8 allspice (whole)
> 8 peppercorns
> 1 laurel leaf
> 3 T cooking oil or fat
> salt to taste
> pepper, for browning

Cut the beef into bite-size chunks. Brown in the oil after seasoning lightly with salt and pepper. Add the sliced onions during the last couple of minutes. Place meat and all other ingredients in a kettle (preferably iron) and stir in the flour and seasonings. Cover with water. Bring to a boil and then cut back the heat and let simmer until meat is tender.

A modern touch calls for the addition of ½ cup of catsup for a more "tomatoey" flavor. A can of tomato soup will produce similar results.

Wild Game Stew (4 servings)

This recipe works well with almost any kind of game, including squirrel, rabbit, venison, etc.

> 2 pounds venison roast, cubed into bite-sized chunks
> 3 T cooking oil
> 3 potatoes, cubed
> 2 medium onions, sliced
> 1 large carrot, sliced
> 1 small rutabaga, cubed
> 1 cup red wine

2 parsley sprigs, chopped
2 T flour
10 peppercorns
salt to taste

Brown the cubed meat in the cooking oil. Add the onion slices during the last couple of minutes. Place meat and onions along with all other ingredients except the parsley, wine and potatoes in a kettle (preferably iron). Stir in the flour. Cover with water. Bring to a boil, then reduce heat and simmer until the meat is tender. When meat starts to get tender, add potatoes and wine. Serve in bowls with the chopped parsley sprinkled on top.

Burbot (eelpout) Stew (4 servings)

Other kinds of fish may be used, but burbot is excellent. Actually, it is a freshwater cousin of the codfish.

2 pounds burbot fillets
1 large onion, chopped
1 large carrot, sliced thin
3 T celery, minced
1 small laurel leaf
6 peppercorns (white)
2 T lemon juice
1½ cups cream
1 T butter, softened
1 T butter, cold
1 T flour

Cut fillets into 1 inch strips (crosswise). Place vegetables in a kettle and cover with water. Add seasonings. Bring to a boil and then reduce heat and let simmer for about 15 minutes. Add fish as well as a mixture of the flour and softened butter. Skim the surface as needed. When the fish flakes easily (about 10 minutes) add the cream. Finally, stir in the cold butter.

Serve over boiled potatoes.

Liver Stew (4 servings)

> 1 pound beef liver
> 3 T flour, lightly seasoned with salt and pepper
> 1 large onion, chopped
> ½ cup chopped mushrooms (your favorite variety)
> 3 T cooking oil
> ½ cup red wine
> 1 t starch
> ½ cup cream
> white pepper and salt to taste

Slice liver. Roll in seasoned flour and sauté along with the onions and mushrooms. Remove liver before it is cooked through. Cut liver slices into bite-size portions. Place liver, onions and mushrooms in a kettle. Cover with water and let simmer, covered, over low heat for ten minutes. Skim as necessary. Stir in wine and starch and continue to simmer another 5 minutes. Stir in the cream. Add salt and pepper to taste.

Serve over potatoes or pasta.

CHAPTER V

FISH

Early Scandinavian immigrants to America told of how sometimes it seemed as though they "lived on fish". Being surrounded by salt water and having an abundance of lakes and streams, this is not surprising. Fish remains a popular food to this day, but unfortunately many of the lakes and streams south of the Arctic Circle are contaminated and the fish are not safe to eat. This is even true of some of the salt water.

It is of interest that two fish Americans often reject, the eel and the eelpout, are truly enjoyed by Scandinavians.

Creamed Dried Fish (4 servings)

> 1½ pounds of dried fish,
> > remove all bones and skin
>
> 2 cups of cream
> 4 T flour
> 4 T butter

Soak the dried fish, with bones and skin removed, for 24 hours. If the fish has also been salted, pour off the water after soaking. Bring to a boil and let simmer for 30 to 45 minutes but not so long that the pieces begin to disintegrate. Cut fish into bite-size pieces. While fish is boiling, prepare a cream sauce from the cream, flour and butter (or use white sauce recipe on next page). Add fish and serve over boiled potatoes.

Lutfisk, poached

Use fish from the market that is presoaked, but soak again for 3-4 hours before cooking. Put enough water in a kettle to completely cover the fish, but do not place the fish in the water until it comes to a rolling boil. Place the pieces of fish in a dish towel or cheesecloth and tie the ends together, like a purse. Submerge the fish in the boiling water. Water will cease boiling. When boiling resumes, remove fish. Beware of over-cooking which will make it like gelatin. Flake the fish away from the skin and bones into a serving dish. Serve with melted butter or a white sauce, usually over potatoes. Season with salt and pepper to taste. (See white sauce recipe below.)

Lutfisk, baked

Use fish that has been presoaked at the market. Soak for another 3-4 hours in cold water before cooking. Place skin-side down (or remove skin) in a buttered baking dish. Lightly season with salt and pepper. Bake in a medium (350°) oven for 30 minutes* or until done (the fish will flake easily with a fork). Flake the fish away from the skin and bones into a serving dish. Serve over potatoes with your favorite sauce or melted butter. Season to taste.

*Large fish may take up to 1 hour.

Suggested sauces for Lutfisk

White Sauce

2 T butter

2 T flour

1 cup milk

a little salt and pepper

2 T lemon juice

Melt the butter—carefully, without burning—in a sauce pan or double boiler. Add the flour and continue to cook for three minutes, stirring continuously. Stir in the lemon juice. Remove pan from the heat and slowly stir in the cup of milk. Return the pan to the stove and bring to a boil, stirring all the while. Place mixture in a double boiler, add salt and pepper, and cook until the sauce thickens. Beat with an egg beater.

Mornay Sauce *

May be used with almost any variety of fish.
Ingredients for about 2 pounds of fillets, steaks or
baked fish:

> 2 T butter
>
> 2 T flour
>
> ½ t seasoned salt
>
> ½ t nutmeg
>
> ½ cup grated Swiss cheese
>
> ½ cup milk
>
> ¼ cup cream
>
> ¼ cup sherry or white wine
>
> 1 t lemon juice

Melt butter; stir in flour; allow to cook a couple of
minutes until it bubbles. Add seasonings, milk, cream
and wine. Stir or whisk to keep smooth and cook until
thick. Add lemon juice and cheese and stir until
blended. Makes about 1¼ cups.

*Courtesy Max Ruttger III, Brainerd, Mn.

Poached Salmon (6 servings)

3 pounds cleaned salmon but with skin on, cut into cross-section chunks (1 to 2 inches thick). Prepare a poaching solution using:

> 2 quarts water
>
> 2 sprigs dill
>
> 6 peppercorns
>
> 1 onion, chopped
>
> 1 T salt

Boil the solution, covered, for about 30 minutes.

Add the salmon chunks and continue to simmer (barely boiling) until done (fish flakes easily). Start checking after 15 minutes and beware of over-cooking.

Serve with dill sauce. (See page 40.)

Baked Whole Fish

> 1 northern pike, 5# or larger
> 6 strips of fat bacon
> 1 onion, sliced
> season to taste

Clean and scale the fish, removing head, fins, entrails, etc. With a knife, make cross-section incisions on the back about 1½ to 2 inches apart, cutting down to the backbone. Rub the inside of the fish with a quartered lemon. Season the inside of the fish with salt and pepper and lightly season the cuts in the back. Lay alternate slices of bacon and onion over the incisions. Bake covered in a medium oven (350⁰) for 45 minutes. Remove the cover and continue baking until the fish at the large end flakes easily with a fork. (Usually another 15 or 20 minutes.)

If you wish to stuff the fish, try this recipe:

> 1 cup raisins
> ¼ lb butter (melted and added to one cup hot water)
> 2 cups croutons or dry bread crumbs
> 1 large onion, chopped but not too fine
> salt and pepper
> ½ cup chopped bologna or sausage

Place the croutons, raisins, meat and onions in a bowl. Salt and pepper lightly while stirring the ingredients together. Stir in the butter-hot water mixture just before stuffing the fish. Lay a sheet of foil on the bottom of the roaster. Stuff the fish (loosely) and place upright on the sheet of foil. Fold the foil up along both sides of the fish to hold in the stuffing.

Panfish with Cream (4 servings)

> 8 panfish (crappies or sunfish work well)
> 1 cup cream
> 4 T butter
> 3 T chopped dill (or 1½ T dill seed)
> 1 lemon, sliced
> salt and pepper to taste

Clean, scale and cut off fins. (Traditional Scandinavian cooking leaves the heads and tails on.) Season inside and out with the salt and pepper. (Lemon-pepper also works well.) Place the fish in a baking dish. Put pats of butter on each fish. Sprinkle fish with chopped dill. Add cream. Cover and bake in a low oven (250-275°). When serving, spoon the cream over the fish and garnish with lemon slices and/or sprigs of dill.

Poached Whitefish (4 servings)

> 2 pounds of whitefish, scaled, cleaned and cut into chunks
>
> 1 onion, sliced
>
> 1 stalk dill (broken)
>
> 2 stalks celery, chopped
>
> 2 T salt
>
> enough water to easily cover the fish pieces plus 2 cups

Place the onion, dill and celery in the water and bring to a boil. Reduce heat and let simmer 30 minutes. Remove 1½ cups of the liquid. Again bring to a boil and place the fish in the liquid. Let boil until fish flakes easily—usually about 15-20 minutes. Meanwhile, prepare a sauce from the following:

> 1½ cups of the fish stock you removed
>
> 1 T butter
>
> 1 T flour
>
> 1 t dill seed
>
> 1 egg, hard-boiled and chopped

Add all ingredients except the egg to the liquid. Let simmer 5 or 6 minutes. Add the chopped egg. Add salt and pepper if needed for your taste. Serve the fish with the sauce, over potatoes or pasta.

Instead of making a sauce, the pieces of fish may be dipped in melted butter and eaten like lobster.

Fried Fish with Cream (4 servings)

> 2 pounds walleye (or other) fillets
>
> cooking oil or butter to fry fish
>
> 1 cup light cream
>
> 2 T chopped chives

2 T chopped cooked beets
2 T parsley, chopped
salt and pepper

Season the fillets (you may lightly coat fillets with flour if you wish) and fry on both sides until brown. Remove the fish and place on a serving platter. Sprinkle the beets, chives and parsley over the fillets. Add the cream to the skillet and bring to a boil. Pour the boiling cream over the fillets.

Chimney Sweepers (4 servings)

8 herring (or stromming)
cooking oil
1 T salt
4 cups salted water (add 3 T salt)

Clean the fish, removing heads, tails and entrails. Rub with salt. Broil on a grill or fry in a hot skillet in oil (on both sides). Dip each fish into the salted water—only for a moment so they do not cool off. Serve with the following sauce, prepared in advance:

1 cup light cream
2 T chopped chives
1 T chopped dill
1 T chopped parsley
1 t white pepper

Mix all of the ingredients into the cream. Serve with the fish and boiled potatoes.

Baked Fillets with Mushrooms (4 servings)

4 fillets (about 2# total weight)—
walleye, northern, etc.
½ pound fresh mushrooms (or ¼ pound canned)
2 T chopped onion
4 T melted butter
2/3 cup bread crumbs
4 T white wine
salt and pepper to taste

Sauté the onion and mushrooms in the butter. Cover the bottom of a baking dish with the onion, mushrooms and butter used for sautéing. Sprinkle the bread crumbs over the mixture; lay the fillets on top, season them lightly. Sprinkle the wine over the fillets (using about half). Bake in a low oven (225⁰) for about 20 minutes or until done. After about 10 minutes, sprinkle the balance of the wine on the fillets. Serve from the baking dish with a spatula.

Fish and Potato Casserole (4 servings)
(called a "pudding" in Scandinavia)

> 2 pounds of fillets. Almost any variety, but salmon and lake trout are especially good.
> 6 potatoes, sliced
> butter, enough to butter the casserole dish
> 3 T chopped dill or 2 T dill seed
> salt and pepper
> 6 eggs
> 1 pint of milk (2 cups)

Butter the casserole dish. Place a layer of sliced potatoes on the bottom. Next a layer of fillets. Lightly season the fillets with salt and pepper. Sprinkle lightly with the dill. Add another layer of potatoes; then a layer of fish, more seasonings, etc. making sure the top layer is potatoes. Beat the eggs and milk together and pour over all. Bake in a low oven (250⁰) for about 1 hour or until potatoes are done.

Fried Filled Herring (4 servings)

> 4 herring or other small fish
> cooking oil or butter
> flour, bread crumbs or cracker crumbs
> salt and pepper

Filling:

> 4 T melted butter
> 4 T parsley, chopped
> 3 T grated horseradish

Fillet the fish (if the fish has scales, scale first). Leave the skin on. Mix the dressing ingredients together. Lightly season the fillets. Spread the dressing on the flesh side of the fillets and put the fillets back together (like a whole fish). You may need to use toothpicks to keep the fillets together. Cover skin sides with breading or flour and fry in a hot skillet.

Fried Fish with Beets and Capers (4 servings)

2 pounds fish fillets (salt or freshwater)
cooking oil or butter
1 cup bread crumbs or cracker crumbs or flour
1 egg, beaten into enough water to dip fillets
salt and pepper
3 T capers
4 T diced pickled beets
1 T parsley and dill, chopped

Dip the fillets in the egg/water mixture, bread, and fry on both sides until brown. Remove the fish and sauté the capers, beets, etc. Pour over the fillets before serving.

Baked Fish with Cheese (4 servings)

8 panfish, herring, perch or other small fish
1 cup grated cheese
1 cup cream
¼ butter, cut into pats
2 tomatoes, sliced
2 T dill, chopped
salt and pepper

Clean the fish (heads, fins, entrails, scale, etc.) Butter a casserole dish. Lightly season fish inside and out. Place the fish side by side, backs up. Panfish may not stand and they may be placed on their sides. If you fillet the fish, stand the fillets of each fish flesh to flesh, as though it were a whole fish. You may need toothpicks to hold the fillets together. Sprinkle the dill and cheese over the fish. Place the pats of butter on the fish. Pour the cream around the fish. Top with the sliced tomatoes. Bake in a low oven (250°) for about 30 minutes.

Fried Salt Herring (4 servings)

8 fillets salt herring
½ cup rye flour (bread crumbs or cracker
        crumbs may be mixed with the flour)
¼ pound butter
2 onions, sliced
1½ cups cream

Bread the herring fillets and brown on both sides in oil or butter. Remove fish from skillet, lay side by side on a platter, and sauté onion slices. Remove slices of onion and place on fillets. Pour cream into same skillet and bring to a boil, stirring all the while. Pour the hot cream over the fillets.

Fried Herring and Mustard (4 servings)

> 8 fresh herring fillets
>
> 3 T prepared mustard
>
> 4 T heavy cream
>
> 2 eggs
>
> 1 cup bread crumbs, flour or cracker crumbs
>
> butter or oil for frying

Beat together the eggs, mustard and cream. Dip fillets in the batter and roll in the crumbs. Fry on both sides until brown. Horseradish may be substituted for the mustard.

Fish Patties with Mushroom Sauce (4 servings)

> 2 pounds ground fish (such as northern pike)
>
> 2 eggs
>
> 2 T minced onion (and/or green pepper)
>
> 1 t white pepper
>
> 2 t salt

Fillet the fish and run it through a meat grinder twice. Thoroughly mix together the ground fish, eggs, onion and seasonings. Form fish into patties and fry in oil or butter or place in a meatloaf pan and bake. If baked, it will take about 1 hour in a 350⁰ oven.

Meanwhile, prepare a mushroom sauce from the following:

> 1 qt fresh mushrooms
>
> butter to sauté mushrooms
>
> 2 T flour
>
> 2 cups cream
>
> salt and pepper to taste

Sauté the mushrooms in the butter. Sprinkle with the flour. Add the cream and cook for about 10 minutes, stirring frequently. Serve over the fish patties.

Torsk (creamed codfish) (4 servings)

2 pounds codfish (half the weight if dried)

1½ cups cream

water

If dried fish is used, soak for 2 hours. Remove skin and bones. Boil in fresh water for 45 minutes. Cut fish into small pieces. Meanwhile, prepare a white sauce according to the recipe on page 36. Serve over potatoes. Season with salt and pepper to taste and top with a large pat of cold butter.

Fillets with Horseradish Tartar Sauce

Fry fish fillets in oil or butter covered with your favorite breading.

Prepare a tartar sauce of the following:

1 cup mayonnaise

2 t prepared horseradish

2 t minced dill (or 1 t dill seed)

Stir together all ingredients and serve with fillets.

Creamed Fish with Horseradish Sauce (4 servings)

2 pounds fillets, cut into 1½ inch chunks

1 lemon, sliced

water

1 T salt

Cover the fillet chunks with water, add the lemon slices and salt, and bring to a boil. Fish should flake easily when done (about 15 minutes). Prepare the sauce from the following ingredients:

1 cup light cream

½ cup water in which fish was boiled

3 T butter

2 T flour

2 T grated horseradish

Melt the butter, stir in the flour, add the fish stock and cream. Place the fish chunks in the sauce and bring to a boil briefly. Remove from heat and stir in the grated horseradish. Serve the fish and the sauce over boiled potatoes. Add a generous pat of cold butter to top off each serving.

Fillets Baked in Cream (4 servings)

> 2 pounds fillets (works well with any white-meated fresh or saltwater fish)
>
> 1 large onion, sliced
>
> 1½ cups cream
>
> 1 T chives, chopped
>
> 1 T dill, chopped
>
> 1 T parsley, chopped
>
> salt and pepper

Grease a baking dish. Lay the onion slices on the bottom of the dish; next, a single layer of fillets. Lightly season with salt and pepper. Cover with cream. Sprinkle on herbs. Bake in medium oven (about 45 minutes).

Eel on straw (4 servings)

> 2 pounds cleaned eel
>
> salt and pepper

Cut eel into serving pieces. Cover the bottom of a baking dish with chopped straw (preferably rye). Lightly season the fish with salt and pepper. Lay the eel on the straw, skin side up. Bake in a medium oven (about 25 minutes). The straw will give a special flavor to the fish.

Crayfish

The crayfish season in Scandinavia usually starts in August and is marked by crayfish parties. Crayfish are really little freshwater cousins of the lobster and taste much the same.

Add generous stalks of dill to salted water and bring to a rolling boil. Drop the crayfish live into the water. When they have turned red they are done. Remove from the water and chill. Serve with melted butter. There is very little meat in the crayfish so cook lots!

CHAPTER VI

MEATS

Scandinavians love their meats. With an abundance of wild game and an historic agricultural economy, this isn't surprising. Even today, more moose are killed by hunters in Sweden than in Alaska!

Scandinavians have extended their smörgasbord tradition to often serving more than one meat dish at a meal—particularly for holidays and celebrations.

Swedish Meatballs #1 (4 servings)

  ½ pound ground beef
  ½ pound ground pork
  ½ cup bread crumbs
  ½ cup cream (half and half will do)
  ½ cup water
  2 T onion, chopped fine
  ½ t salt
  ½ t pepper
  1 t allspice
  1 egg
  butter for frying

Thoroughly blend the beef and pork, work in the seasonings, a little at a time for a thorough blend. Mix together the bread crumbs, cream and water and blend in. Beat the egg and work that into the mixture. Work into balls (small for hors d' oeuvres, large for a meal). Fry one first to check seasoning, then do the balance. Fry in a heavy skillet over moderate heat. Be sure they are done thoroughly.

Swedish Meatballs #2

1 pound ground beef
1 large onion, chopped fine
1 cup bread crumbs
1 cup light cream
1 egg
salt and pepper to taste
butter or oil for frying

Sauté the chopped onion. Soak the bread crumbs in the cream. Beat the egg. Mix together all ingredients. Fry a small meatball to check seasoning. Use a heavy skillet and fry over medium heat. When done through, remove meatballs from skillet and make a gravy, as follows:

Work 1 T flour into the pan drippings. Add 1 bouillon cube to 2 cups of water. Add to the pan. Stir over low heat until desired consistency (usually 8-10 minutes). Add a little salt and pepper to taste. Serve gravy over meatballs and/or potatoes.

Roast Ham (fresh) (8 servings)

1 fresh ham
Marinade consisting of the following ingredients:
2 large onions, sliced
1 laurel leaf
6 cloves
10 peppercorns
10 whole allspice
1 cup celery, chopped
2 medium carrots, sliced thin
2 cups red wine
3 T lemon juice
4 T brown sugar
3 T prepared mustard
1 cup water
2 T vinegar (preferably wine vinegar)

Score the ham with a knife (traditionally in diamond shapes). Place in a suitable container. Mix together all ingredients for the marinade and pour over the ham. Let stand, refrigerated, 48 hours. Turn every 12 hours. Roast in a medium oven, basting every 30 minutes with marinade. A gravy may be made by adding flour and cream to the pan juices. Do not use the left-over marinade unless you boil it first.

Veal Roast with Dill Sauce (6 servings)

> 3-4 pound veal roast
>
> salt and pepper

Lightly season the roast and place it in a roaster that has been well greased with butter. Bake in a medium oven for about one hour; do not over-roast. A meat thermometer is helpful. Meanwhile, prepare dill sauce as follows and serve over sliced roast.

> 2 T minced fresh dill or 1 T dry dill
>
> 1 T chopped onion
>
> 2 T butter
>
> 1 T flour
>
> 1 cup cream
>
> salt and pepper to taste

Sauté the onion pieces until clear. Stir in flour and cook for 3 minutes. Stir in all other ingredients, seasoning to taste. Serve over sliced roast.

Brisket of Veal with Dill Sauce (4 servings)

> 2 pounds cheaper cuts of veal, sliced serving size
>
> water to cover meat
>
> 10 peppercorns
>
> 2 stalks dill, broken
>
> 1 stalk celery, chopped
>
> 1 bay leaf
>
> 1 onion, sliced
>
> 4 cloves
>
> 1 T salt

Place sliced veal in a skillet. Cover with water. Add all ingredients. Bring to a boil and then reduce heat and let simmer for one hour or until tender. Skim regularly. Meanwhile, prepare dill sauce as above.

Beef Roast/Pork Roast (8-10 servings)

Roasting beef and pork in the same pan gives each meat a special flavor.

> 3 pound beef roast
> 3 pound pork roast
> 1 large onion, sliced
> 2 large carrots, chunked
> 8 peppercorns
> salt and pepper for gravy
> cooking oil

Lightly season roasts with salt and pepper. Place cooking oil in heavy skillet and brown roasts on all sides. Pour oil used in browning roasts into a roasting pan. Place both roasts in pan, scattering vegetables and seasonings on and around roasts. Bake in low oven (250^0). Turn roasts occasionally. When roasts are done, work in a little flour and stir in water or milk to make gravy. Season gravy with salt and pepper to taste.

Roast Moose (6 servings)

> 4-5 pound moose roast (with all fat removed)
> 3 strips fat bacon
> salt and pepper
> 1 cup red wine

Season the roast on all sides. Cut the bacon strips into 1 inch pieces. Cut slits in roast and insert bacon pieces (to moisten the roast). Pour the wine into a roasting pan and place the roast in the pan. Bake in a low (250^0) oven. Serve on hot plates.

Rolled Sidepork

> 2 pounds lean sidepork, fresh
> 1 T allspice (whole)
> 1 T peppercorns (preferably white)
> 1½ T salt

Make the sidepork half as thick by slicing through the meat horizontally, but don't quite cut all the way through—leave enough so that the two halves hang together. Crush the spices. Spread the meat out and evenly distribute the spices. Roll the meat tightly, with the rind side out. Tie the roll in several places with string. Place in a deep pan. Cover with water seasoned with the following:

> 10 whole allspice
>
> 10 peppercorns
>
> 2 T salt
>
> 1 bay leaf

Bring to a boil, then reduce heat and let simmer (covered) for 2 hours. Remove from liquid, refrigerate (covered) overnight. Serve cold, sliced.

Reindeer Sausage (patties)

> 20 pounds dressed wild game
>
> 10 pounds fat pork (this amount will vary with taste, but unless you use at least this weight of fat pork the sausage will be dry)
>
> 2 t sugar
>
> 1 t ginger
>
> ½ pound fine salt
>
> 2 T pepper
>
> 1 T sage

Cut the meat up into small pieces which can be easily fed into a grinder. Run the meat through the grinder twice. To assure uniform seasoning, place the ground meat into five or more piles and work the proportionate amount of seasoning in with your hands. Form into patties and refrigerate or divide into approximately 1 pound quantities, wrap in freezer paper and freeze.

Roasted Spare Ribs (4 servings)

> 3 pounds spare ribs
>
> 1 T ginger
>
> 1 T salt
>
> ½ T pepper

Mix together the spices and rub the meat. Roast in a low oven (225⁰) fat side up for 1½ hours. A gravy may be made from the drippings by working in flour and then adding water. Or stir the flour into the water first and then add the mixture a little at a time while continually stirring (over heat).

Jellied Veal and Pork (sylta)

                3 pounds veal (neck, breast or shank)
                1 pound pork (shank or other cheap cut)
                ¼ t ginger
                ¼ t salt
                ¼ t pepper (white)
                water (a quart and one-half)

Cover the meat (in a kettle) with the water. Bring to a boil, reduce heat and let simmer for a couple of hours. Skim regularly. Remove from heat but save liquid. Remove meat, pick from bones, and chop into small pieces. Meanwhile, return liquid to heat and boil down about one-third. Remove from heat and strain. Add seasonings and meat to the liquid* and return to heat; bringing it briefly to a boil, pour into loaf pans or other appropriate mold. Refrigerate. Serve sliced.

*If the liquid does not cover all the meat, add water.

Fried Duck (4 servings)

                2 wild ducks
                1 slice lard or animal fat (may substitute butter)
                2 T butter
                salt and pepper

Clean and thoroughly wash bird, inside and out. Season inside and out with salt and pepper. Tie the lard to the breast or rub with butter. Place 2 T butter in iron kettle. Tie up bird (wings and legs) with string. Fry in covered kettle over medium heat. Turn and baste occasionally. Continue frying until done—usually less than 1 hour. Remove birds and add ½ cup water, 1½ cups cream, 2 T melted butter, and 2 T flour to the drippings. Stir as you continue to heat until the gravy has the "right" consistency. Season with salt and pepper to taste.

Grouse and Veal (4 servings)

                2 grouse, ground
                ¾ pound veal, ground
                ½ pound lard, ground (or substitute melted butter)
                4 eggs
                1 cup bread crumbs
                ½ t pepper
                ½ t salt

Cut all meat from the grouse. Run the grouse, veal and lard through a meat grinder (fine). Mix together all ingredients. If lard was not used, add melted butter at this point. Blend ingredients evenly. Form into meatballs. Place in a covered, buttered, oven dish and bake at 350⁰, basting several times. Serve with a white sauce. (see page 36).

Pot Roast (6 servings)

> 4 pound roast (beef or wild game)
> ½ cup cooking oil
> ½ t salt
> ½ t pepper

Rub roast with salt and pepper. Add oil to an iron kettle. Brown the roast on all sides over medium heat. Add 1 cup water. Cover and roast over low heat (200⁰). Vegetables, such as potatoes, carrots and parsnips, may be cooked with the roast. Add them after the meat has been browned.

For a gravy, boil stock down to about 1 cup. Add 6 T melted butter, 4 T flour, and 2 cups cream. Season to taste. For browner gravy, add a little soy sauce or Kitchen Bouquet. Cook down to desired thickness, stirring all the while.

Roast Duck or Goose

Thoroughly clean duck or goose, inside and out. Rub inside and out with salt and pepper.

Stuff bird with quartered apples and prunes (half of each). Sew or fasten openings. Roast, covered, in a medium oven. Add a cup of water or red wine to the bottom of the roasting pan.

Meanwhile, boil the giblets until tender; it takes longer for the gizzards than for the hearts or livers. When done, remove from liquid and chop fine to be used in the gravy. When the birds are done, remove from pan. Spoon off excess grease. Return giblets to the roasting pan. Sprinkle on some flour. Add water, a little at a time, and continue to heat, stirring all the while. Be careful that gravy does not get too thick. Season to taste.

Spiced Tongue

For two small or one large tongue:

1 T salt
4 whole black peppers
6 whole cloves
4 whole allspice
1 bay leaf (large)
1 T vinegar
1 small onion, sliced

Cover tongues with water. Simmer for one hour. Add all other ingredients and simmer for another hour or two until tender. Cool. Slit skin on underside of tongues and peel off. Slice on a slant.

Potato Sausage (Potatis Korv)*

3 pounds ground pork (lean)
2 pounds lean ground beef
10 pounds potatoes
2 T pepper
5 T salt
1½ t allspice (ground)
1½ t ginger
½ pound casings

Soak casings in water to soften and remove salt. Peel and grind potatoes, using medium blade. Add meat and seasonings. Mix well. Tie end of casing and *loosely* fill in 24" lengths—tie open ends. (The sausage expands when cooked). Keep covered with water. Prick in several places before cooking. Simmer for 30 - 45 minutes. Drain off water and sauté slowly until browned.

Uncooked potato sausage may be frozen in airtight zip-locked bags. Exposure to air causes the potatoes to discolor.

*Courtesy Karen Anderson Cowie

Pickled Tongue (or heart)

For 4 to 6 deer tongues:

1 pt vinegar

1 pt water

2 T sugar

1 t whole cloves

1 t whole allspice

1 t whole black peppers

¼ t mustard seed

½ t salt

Wash tongues in salted water. Place in fresh water. Add 1 tablespoon allspice and let simmer one to two hours or until tender. (It will never get real tender.) Let cool and peel off skin and cut off root ends. Place in jars and submerge in a pickling solution prepared from the above ingredients which has been boiled for about 10 minutes.

Refrigerate and let stand one week before eating.

Liver Sausage

1 pound sliced liver, smoked*

1 onion, sliced

1 carrot, sliced

¼ t fresh ground black peppercorns

½ T garlic salt

2 T salt (level)

2 T wheat germ

powdered milk

Sauté the onion slices until transparent (preferably in bacon grease). Add liver, carrots, pepper and garlic (and more oil if necessary) and cook until liver is cooked and carrots are soft (about 10 or 12 minutes). Run the mixture through a meat grinder two or three times until smooth and well blended. Add the remaining ingredients, using enough powdered milk to make a firm mixture. Wrap in plastic or sausage casings and refrigerate. Use as a paste on crackers or slice as a sandwich meat.

* If smoked liver is not available, use fresh and add 1 T smoke flavoring.

Head Cheese

This tasty delicacy receives its name from the fact that pork used traditionally came from a hog's head. You may still use that source for this recipe, but hogs' heads may be a little hard to come by in your local market!

>   4 lbs pork shoulder roast or lean meat from a
>   hog's head
>   10 allspice (whole)
>   5 bay leaves
>   1 t garlic salt
>   1 t white pepper
>   3 T brown sugar
>   2 onions, sliced (medium)
>   2 T salt

Chop the pork into small pieces (about ½ bite-size).

Place in a pot and cover with water. Bring to a boil, then reduce heat and let simmer on low until very tender (about 4-5 hours).

Place the meat in a dishtowel; tie with a string and place in a stone crock or other non-metallic container.

Make a spice-brine by adding the spices and brown sugar as listed above to enough water to cover the meat. Boil briefly, stirring continuously. Pour the solution over the meat.

Place a board on top of the meat and press down firmly. Place a clean rock on top of the board to maintain pressure.

Store in a cool place or under refrigeration. Wait a couple of days and then slice cold to serve—with vinegar on the side.

Meat Roll (rullepolse)

Flank meat or other relatively thin "sheets" of meat that can be rolled are usually used. Meat scraps that would normally be used for stew meat (or hamburger) are also used (not tough pieces, however). All meat should be boneless.

Lay the flank meat flat. Spread the scraps (bite-sized) evenly over the flank meat. Season lightly with salt and pepper. Sprinkle 1/3 teaspoon ginger to each pound of meat. Chop a large onion and sprinkle over meat. Roll and wrap tightly with string.

Prepare a brine solution with enough water to cover the meat. Use enough salt to float an egg or a potato. Add ½ teaspoon saltpeter per gallon of water. Boil until the salt dissolves.

When the brine has cooled, place the meat roll in a non-metallic container and cover with the solution. Place a weight on top to keep the meat totally submerged. Let soak in cool place 48 hours. Remove and soak overnight in fresh water in a cool place.

Remove and place in fresh water again and boil slowly for two hours.

Place meat in loaf pan; force to fit. Use more than one pan and cut meat to fit if necessary. Store in cool place with weight on top to hold shape.

Slice thin and serve cold.

Pork with Apples

> 2 pounds pork steak
> 6 apples
> salt and pepper
> butter
> water

Peel and core the apples, then slice them. Lightly season the pork steak. Butter the bottom of a baking dish. Place a layer of apple slices on the bottom of the dish, then a layer of steak. Add another layer of apple slices and another layer of steaks, etc. Slice more apples if necessary, ending with apples as the top layer. Cover with water, barely covering the top layer of steaks and leaving the top layer of apples uncovered. Bake in medium oven until tender.

Pan-fried Steak and Onions

> 2 pounds beef steak
> 4 onions, sliced
> salt and pepper
> 4 T butter

Sauté the onion slices in an iron frying pan. Lightly season the steaks. Remove the onions and fry the steaks on a hot stove. If you have doubts about the tenderness of the steaks, before frying pound them with the butt of a knife or even work in a little flour as you pound them. Serve the steaks piping hot with the onion slices on top.

CHAPTER VII

VEGETABLES, CASSEROLES AND SIDE DISHES

Sometimes visitors to Scandinavia say that the only vegetable they see is potatoes! Really not true, but potatoes are traditionally a very important part of the Scandinavian diet. But so is cabbage and so are beets—and the other vegetables common to America.

Scandinavians are skilled at combining meats and fish with vegetables in casseroles and in side dishes.

Potato-Sausage Dinner in a Frying Pan (4 servings)

> 1 pound ground sausage or sausage in casings, cooked
> 4 large potatoes, boiled and sliced
> 1 medium onion, chopped
> 3 T green pepper, chopped
> 3 T butter
> salt and pepper to taste

Boil the sausages or fry the ground sausage. Boil the potatoes (leave skins on if they are new potatoes) until they are easily penetrated with a fork, but do not over-cook. Slice the potatoes. If sausage in casings is used, slice about 1/3 inch thick. Almost any kind of sausage works well; it just depends on your taste whether you want a spicy or a mild dish. Melt the butter in an iron skillet, add all ingredients and stir together. Stir occasionally (over medium heat) so as not to burn. Serve when all ingredients are piping hot.

Root-moos (rutabagas and potatoes)

Use equal portions (by volume) of rutabagas and potatoes. Cover with water, add a dash of salt and boil together until soft enough to mash. Remove from the water and mash them together. Add a pat of butter from time to time and mash and stir until thoroughly blended. Add salt and pepper to taste. Serve as a vegetable with the meal.

Salt Pork and Cabbage (serves 6)

>1 pound salt pork
>1 medium head of cabbage
>4 potatoes (medium)
>1 large onion
>6 peppercorns (preferably white)
>1 laurel leaf or ½ bay leaf
>4 whole cloves
>1 t salt

Remove any rind from the pork and cut into bite-size cubes. Cover with water in a kettle large enough to hold all ingredients. Bring to a boil, cover, reduce heat, and let simmer 15 minutes. Meanwhile, cut the head of cabbage into narrow wedges (about 2 inches thick at the outside of the wedge). Slice the onion, and peel and cube the potatoes (bite-size). Skim the surface of the water of anything that may have come to the top. Place all of the ingredients on top of the pork; add water if necessary so that all of the ingredients are covered. Cook until tender. The dish may be served as a soup or the water poured off and served as a side dish.

Creamed Spinach (serves 6)

>1 pound spinach (fresh or frozen)
>2 cups cream (or half and half)
>2 T butter
>1 T flour
>salt and pepper to taste

After cleaning the spinach and removing any parts that may not be tender, cover the spinach with water and boil until wilted. Remove spinach and chop coarsely. Add the butter to a frying pan, melt, and then sauté the spinach briefly, sprinkling with the flour. Stir in the cream gradually, and season to taste.

Boiled Potatoes with Dill

Use small, new potatoes. Scrub clean. Cover with water, add a little salt and a few sprigs of fresh dill, and boil until done.

Serve with butter, or with milk seasoned with pepper and chopped chives as a gravy.

Boiled Potatoes with Butter and Parsley

Use small, new potatoes (either peel or leave jackets on). Boil in salted water until tender. Drain and place in a bowl. Drizzle melted butter and sprinkle chopped parsley over the potatoes before serving.

Swedish Brown Beans

> 1 pound dried brown beans
> 6 cups water
> 3 T vinegar (or 4 T catsup)
> 1 T salt
> 3 T syrup

Soak beans in water for 12 hours. Leaving beans in the water in which they have been soaking, add salt and bring to a boil. Cover, reduce heat and let simmer 2½ hours. Stir in syrup and vinegar or catsup. Start with less, add more if it suits your taste. Small cubes of pork may be added during the boiling process.

Glorified Rice (serves 6)

> 1 cup white rice
> 1 cup whipping cream, whipped
> (add sugar to taste)
> 1 small can crushed pineapple
> 2 cups water
> 2 T butter
> 2 T sugar
> salt to taste (start with ½ t)

Bring the water to a boil in a saucepan. Add the rice and butter. Let simmer about 20 minutes, covered. Let cool. Stir in the salt, whipped cream, pineapple and additional sugar to taste.

The cream may be added following cooking and served as a hot side dish.

Vegetables in a White Sauce

Cook the vegetables (carrots, peas, etc.) in salted water until tender. Meanwhile, prepare a white sauce from the following ingredients:

> 3 T flour
>
> 1½ T butter
>
> 1½ cups milk
>
> ½ cup liquid in which the vegetables were cooked
>
> salt and pepper (white) to taste
>
> 4 T parsley, chopped, for garnish

Melt butter; stir in the flour. Add the liquids and bring to a boil, beating until smooth. Reduce heat and let simmer a few minutes. Season to taste. Add the vegetables. Sprinkle chopped parsley on surface just before serving.

Cabbage Rolls (6 servings)

> ½ cup rice
>
> 1 cup onion, chopped
>
> 1 head cabbage, medium
>
> 1½ pounds ground beef
>
> 1½ cups tomato juice
>
> 1 T Worcestershire sauce
>
> 1 T sour cream (from the dairy case)
>
> salt and pepper
>
> Cook the rice.

Wash the cabbage. Take out the center core. Place the head in hot water until the leaves start to loosen or become limp. Carefully separate off a dozen of the larger leaves. Mix together the hamburger, rice, onion, sour cream, Worcestershire sauce and season lightly. Place about a third of a cup of the mixture on each leaf, as far as it will go. Roll up in each cabbage leaf and pin with toothpicks. Cover the bottom of the baking dish with cabbage leaves and then lay the cabbage rolls on this bed of leaves. Pour the tomato juice over the cabbage rolls and place in a 325⁰ oven. Bake for about one hour and fifteen minutes. Remove the rolls and place on a serving platter. Pour the tomato juice over the rolls. If you wish, you may thicken the juice by stirring in a little flour.

CHAPTER VIII

DESSERTS

Scandinavian goodies and desserts have become very popular in the United States at Christmas time and have become a good counter-balance to the negative feelings some people have towards two other traditional Scandinavian holiday foods: lefse and lutfisk! Unfortunately, Scandinavian desserts often feature heavy cream and lots of butter. Lighter dairy products may be substituted, however, and the treats will still taste great.

Crullers (about 3 dozen)

        3 egg yolks

        2 cups flour

        4 T sugar

        4 T cream

        2 T butter, softened

        1 T finely grated lemon or orange peel

        optional: 2 T brandy or cognac

Mix together all ingredients, thoroughly, adding the flour last. Work into a dough; refrigerate 3 hours. Roll the dough into a thin sheet, no more than ¼ inch. Cut the sheet of dough into strips about 3 inches long and ½ inch wide. Make a slit in the middle of each piece (about 1 inch long). Pull one end of each strip through the slit. Cook in hot oil until crispy-brown. Sprinkle with sugar (regular or powdered).

Jelly Roll

2 eggs
1 cup flour
2 T butter, melted
½ cup sugar
2 T starch
¼ cup hot water
1 t baking powder
jam filling of your choice

Beat the eggs and sugar until fluffy; add water and beat another minute. Mix together the flour, starch and baking powder. Sift into the liquid and stir in. Place waxed paper on a cookie sheet. Spread the dough evenly on the waxed paper (about ½ inch thick) and bake in a hot oven (about 450^0) for about 5 minutes or until brown. Remove from oven. Spread out another piece of waxed paper; sprinkle sugar on it. Turn the cake onto the paper with sugar on it. Remove the top paper (the first paper) and spread the cake with a layer of preserves of your choosing. Roll the cake up and let cool. Scandinavians traditionally served the jelly roll with whipped cream.

Rhubarb Cake

2 cups rhubarb, cleaned, scraped and cut into
    ½ inch chunks
2 eggs
4 T butter, melted
4 T sugar
1½ cups flour
3 cups milk
dash of salt

Sauté the rhubarb briefly in the melted butter. Spread evenly over the bottom of a greased baking dish. Meanwhile, combine all other ingredients into a batter. Pour the batter over the rhubarb. Bake in a medium oven. Serve with whipped cream topping or sprinkle with sugar while the cake is still hot.

Stuffed Apples

    4 large apples (preferably a hard variety)
    your favorite jam
    3 eggs, separated
    3 T sugar
    2 T ground nuts (of your choice)

Peel and core the apples. Stuff them with the jam. Beat the egg yolks and sugar together. Beat the whites until stiff and add to the yolks. Pour over apples and then sprinkle each apple with the ground nuts. Bake in a 400⁰ oven for about 20 minutes.

Rosettes *

shortening for frying
batter:
2 eggs
2 T sugar
¼ t salt
1 cup milk
1 cup sifted flour

Beat eggs, adding milk and flour alternately until batter is smooth. Add sugar and salt. Have rosette iron hot. Dip iron into batter and then into hot oil. Let fry until golden brown.

*Courtesy Avis Sandland, Clearbrook, Mn.

Filbunke (fermented milk)

    1 quart milk
    6 T fermented milk
    6 T heavy cream

Heat the milk to the boiling point, then remove from heat and let cool to room temperature. Stir in fermented milk and cream. Pour into serving bowls; let stand overnight. Refrigerate before serving. Sprinkle nutmeg on surface.

Fruit Soup

Fruit soup may be served either at the start of the meal or as a dessert or even for breakfast.

> 2 quarts water
> ½ cup raisins
> 1 cup prunes, sliced
> 1 cup apricots, sliced (or peaches or other fruit)
> juice of ½ orange
> juice of ½ lemon
> ½ cup sugar
> ½ cup tapioca
> ½ t salt
> 1 stick cinnamon

Place the fruit in the water; bring to a boil and then reduce heat and let simmer about 20 minutes. Let cool. Add all other ingredients and cook until the tapioca is transparent. Serve hot or cold.

Prune Tarts

> 3 cups flour
> 1½ cups whipping cream
> ½ t salt
> 1 T baking powder
> ½ pound butter, softened
> 1 pound prunes
> ½ cup sugar
> 1 T lemon juice

Whip the cream. Prepare the dough by mixing together the flour, salt and baking powder and sifting it into the cream. Stir thoroughly and then blend in the softened butter. Refrigerate dough 2 hours.

Cover prunes with water and cook until soft. Drain, remove pits, and place in a blender until of a purée consistency. Mix sugar and lemon juice into the prunes.

Roll the dough into a sheet about 1/3 inch thick. Cut into 3 inch squares. Cut the corner of each square halfway to the center. Place a tablespoon of prune purée in the center of each square.

Bring half of each split corner over the prune filling towards the center of the square. Place tarts on an ungreased cookie sheet. Let stand while you preheat the oven to 400⁰. Bake until brown—about 12 minutes.

Kringla (cookies)

4 cups flour

1 t baking powder

1 t baking soda

1½ cups sugar

½ t salt

1 cup milk (buttermilk preferred)

½ pound butter, softened

1 egg

2 t vanilla

Mix together the dry ingredients. Add the milk, butter and vanilla. Mix (electric mixer) at low speed until thoroughly blended. Add egg and continue mixing a couple more minutes. Refrigerate dough (cover mixing bowl) for 2 hours. On lightly floured breadboard, mold dough into 1 inch balls. Roll each ball to form a rope about 6 inches long. Form each rope into a figure eight. Bake in a preheated 375⁰ oven until edges are hard and a light brown. If you want to keep them soft, sprinkle with water before storing.

Glöög (A beverage served on winter holidays and special occasions)

1 bottle red wine

1/3 cup vodka (or schnapps)

1 whole ginger root

2 sticks cinnamon

½ t cardamon seed

8 cloves (whole)

Bring almost to a boil. Pour into mugs over 1 T seedless raisins and 3 blanched almonds. Serve piping hot.

Bread Pudding

2 cups bread crumbs (either white or rye)
1 cup apples, grated or finely chopped
juice of 1 orange
4 T sugar
1 cup whipping cream

Whip the cream and set it aside. Mix together all ingredients except the orange juice. Add this a little at a time, stirring it in (to prevent soaking just a part of the mixture). Serve topped with the whipped cream.

Lingonberry Sauce

Use 1¼ pounds of sugar to every 2 pounds of berries. Add sugar a little at a time, stirring and crushing the berries at the same time. When the sugar has been dissolved and the berries are a juicy pulp, they are ready to be served. Serve chilled.

Rømme Grøt*

1 qt thick sweet cream
1 cup flour
2 cups warm milk
1 t salt
cinnamon and sugar to sprinkle on top

Bring cream to a boil for about 15 minutes. Gradually sift flour into the cream, mix with a wire whip until very smooth. Allow to simmer, skimming off the fat as it separates. After most of the fat has been skimmed off, add the warm milk and stir until smooth. Add the salt. Pour into bowls and sprinkle top with sugar and cinnamon. Pour the fat over it.

*Courtesy Avis Sandland, Clearbrook, Mn.